PRINCEWILL LAGANG

Google's Co-founder: Sergey Brin's Journey from Code to Canvas

First published by PRINCEWILL LAGANG 2023

Copyright © 2023 by Princewill Lagang

All rights reserved. No part of this publication may be reproduced, stored or transmitted in any form or by any means, electronic, mechanical, photocopying, recording, scanning, or otherwise without written permission from the publisher. It is illegal to copy this book, post it to a website, or distribute it by any other means without permission.

Princewill Lagang asserts the moral right to be identified as the author of this work.

First edition

This book was professionally typeset on Reedsy. Find out more at reedsy.com

Contents

1	Introduction	1
2	A Silicon Valley Genesis	2
3	The Google Odyssey: Scaling the Peaks of Innovation	5
4	Moonshots and Beyond: Sergey Brin's Visionary Quest	8
5	The Philosopher Coder: Sergey Brin's Ethical Stance in the...	11
6	Sergey Brin: A Personal Odyssey Beyond Technology	14
7	Sergey Brin's Vision for Tomorrow: Navigating the Future...	17
8	Sergey Brin's Cultural Impact: Redefining Innovation and...	20
9	Sergey Brin: A Continuum of Curiosity and Impact	23
10	Sergey Brin's Visionary Tapestry: Weaving Innovation into...	26
11	Sergey Brin: A Reflection on Innovation, Impact, and the...	29
12	Beyond the Horizon: The Ongoing Legacy of Sergey Brin	32
13	The Future Unveiled: Sergey Brin's Enduring Vision for...	35
14	Summary	38

1

Introduction

Welcome to the enthralling exploration of "Sergey Brin: A Journey of Innovation and Impact." In this narrative, we embark on a voyage through the life and legacy of Sergey Brin, the co-founder of Google, as we unravel the intricacies of his remarkable journey in the world of technology. From his early days as a passionate coder to his role in shaping one of the most influential companies in the digital era, we delve into the key chapters that define Brin's impact on the tech industry, his ethical considerations, personal pursuits, and his visionary perspective on the future. Join us as we unveil the layers of a tech pioneer's narrative, celebrating innovation, ethical leadership, and the ongoing exploration of uncharted frontiers.

2

A Silicon Valley Genesis

Title: "Google's Co-founder: Sergey Brin's Journey from Code to Canvas"

In the bustling landscape of Silicon Valley, where innovation is the heartbeat of the region, a brilliant mind emerged to redefine the digital era. Sergey Brin, one of the masterminds behind Google, embarked on a transformative journey that transcended the boundaries of code and ventured into the realm of creativity – a journey from the binary world of algorithms to the vivid canvas of innovation.

Section 1: Inception

The Silicon Valley Crucible

The chapter opens with a vivid description of the Silicon Valley ecosystem, exploring its unique blend of ambition, talent, and relentless pursuit of technological advancement. It sets the stage for the birth of a visionary mind and introduces readers to the landscape that shaped Sergey Brin's early years.

A Russian Roots Prelude

Delve into Brin's cultural background, tracing his roots to Russia. Explore the impact of his family's emigration to the United States and the values instilled in him during his formative years. The narrative highlights the intersection of his Russian heritage with the American Dream, laying the groundwork for Brin's later pursuits.

Section 2: A Curious Mind

The Stanford Connection

Transitioning into Brin's academic journey, the narrative unfolds at Stanford University, the epicenter of technological innovation. Dive into the corridors of Stanford's Computer Science department, exploring Brin's early experiences, the intellectual atmosphere, and the serendipitous meeting that would change the course of his life.

The Catalyst: Larry Page

Introduce Larry Page, Brin's fellow Stanford Ph.D. student, and explore the chemistry that ignited their partnership. Detail their initial collaborations, the shared vision that bonded them, and the seeds of Google's inception that were planted in the rich soil of academic curiosity.

Section 3: From Code to Concept

The Birth of Google

Chronicle the pivotal moments leading to the birth of Google. Explore the dorm room brainstorming sessions, the coding marathons, and the breakthroughs that propelled Brin and Page from being ambitious students to pioneers of the search engine revolution. Uncover the challenges they faced and the innovative solutions that became the bedrock of Google.

The Code that Changed Everything

Delve into the technical nuances of the PageRank algorithm, the groundbreaking innovation that fueled Google's rise. Break down complex concepts into accessible explanations, allowing readers to grasp the genius behind the code that reshaped the digital landscape.

Section 4: Beyond Bits and Bytes

From Search to Innovation

Shift the narrative from the technical to the visionary as Brin and Page transition from building a search engine to envisioning a company that transcends the limitations of traditional tech enterprises. Explore their commitment to innovation, user-centric design, and the principles that laid the foundation for Google's evolution.

A Glimpse of the Future

Conclude the chapter by foreshadowing the themes that will be explored further in the book. From the birth of Google to the evolving role of technology in society, Sergey Brin's journey serves as a microcosm of the digital revolution, offering insights into the past, present, and future of innovation.

Chapter 1 sets the stage for a captivating exploration of Sergey Brin's multifaceted journey, inviting readers to witness the fusion of code and canvas that defines the legacy of one of Silicon Valley's most enigmatic figures.

3

The Google Odyssey: Scaling the Peaks of Innovation

Section 1: Building the Foundation

The Garage Office

Open the chapter with a glimpse into Google's humble beginnings, exploring the garage-turned-office that housed the burgeoning company. Detail the challenges Brin and Page faced as they transitioned from academia to entrepreneurship, emphasizing their resourcefulness and determination to turn their vision into reality.

From Garage to Googleplex

Trace Google's growth trajectory, from the makeshift office to the sprawling Googleplex headquarters. Explore the milestones, partnerships, and key hires that propelled the company forward. Highlight the unique culture that emerged within Google, emphasizing its emphasis on innovation, collaboration, and employee well-being.

Section 2: The Rise of Google

Search Domination

Examine Google's ascent to search engine dominance. Dive into the strategies employed to refine and improve the search algorithm continually. Explore the impact of Google's user-centric approach and the relentless pursuit of delivering the most relevant results, solidifying its position as the go-to search engine.

Monetizing Innovation

Shift the narrative to Google's monetization strategies, exploring the introduction of AdWords and AdSense. Analyze how Brin and Page transformed the advertising landscape, blending innovation with profitability. Delve into the challenges and ethical considerations associated with monetizing a platform that had become an integral part of the digital experience.

Section 3: Google's Ecosystem Expansion

Beyond Search: Product Diversification

Explore Google's foray into diverse product offerings beyond its core search functionality. Detail the introduction of Gmail, Google Maps, and Google News, showcasing the company's commitment to providing a comprehensive digital experience. Examine how each product contributed to Google's expanding ecosystem.

The Android Revolution

Zoom in on Google's strategic move into the mobile space with the development of the Android operating system. Unpack the motivations behind this bold venture, the challenges faced, and the transformative impact it had on the smartphone industry. Highlight how Google's influence extended beyond the digital realm and into the physical world.

Section 4: Challenges and Controversies

Privacy Concerns and Ethical Dilemmas

Confront the ethical challenges and controversies that accompanied Google's rapid expansion. Explore issues related to user privacy, data collection, and the ethical implications of Google's growing influence. Scrutinize how the company navigated these challenges while striving to maintain user trust and societal responsibility.

Anti-Trust Scrutiny

Examine Google's encounters with anti-trust investigations and legal challenges. Unpack the complexities of these regulatory issues, detailing the allegations, investigations, and the evolving landscape of technology regulation. Discuss how these challenges shaped Google's corporate strategy and its approach to competition.

Section 5: A Changing of the Guard

Alphabet Inc.: Restructuring the Future

Detail the restructuring of Google into Alphabet Inc. Explore the motivations behind this significant organizational shift, the redefinition of Google's role within the larger corporate structure, and the implications for Brin and Page's leadership. Analyze how this strategic move positioned Google for future growth and innovation.

The Evolution of Leadership

Conclude the chapter by examining the evolving roles of Sergey Brin and Larry Page within Alphabet Inc. Explore their pursuits beyond Google, such as involvement in moonshot projects and philanthropy. Highlight how their leadership style adapted to the changing landscape of technology and innovation.

Chapter 2 unfolds as an epic journey through Google's evolution, from a garage start-up to a global powerhouse. It explores the triumphs, challenges, and transformative moments that define the company's legacy, all against the backdrop of Sergey Brin's relentless pursuit of innovation.

4

Moonshots and Beyond: Sergey Brin's Visionary Quest

S ection 1: The X Lab: Where Moonshots Take Flight

The Birth of Google X

Open the chapter with an exploration of Google X, the secretive research lab where ambitious and audacious projects, known as moonshots, come to life. Delve into the culture of experimentation, risk-taking, and the pursuit of groundbreaking ideas that defined the X Lab. Highlight how Sergey Brin's passion for pushing boundaries played a pivotal role in the creation of Google X.

Project Loon: Connecting the Unconnected

Zoom in on one of the early moonshot projects, Project Loon, which aimed to provide internet access to remote and underserved areas using high-altitude balloons. Explore the technical challenges, the global impact, and the lessons learned from this endeavor. Illustrate how Brin's commitment to leveraging technology for social good manifested in projects like Project Loon.

Section 2: Google Glass: Through the Eyes of Innovation

The Vision for Wearable Technology

Transition to the development of Google Glass, a groundbreaking foray into wearable technology. Explore Brin's vision for a hands-free, augmented reality experience and the challenges faced in bringing this futuristic device to the consumer market. Examine the public reception, the controversies surrounding privacy, and the eventual discontinuation of Google Glass.

Lessons from Glass

Reflect on the lessons learned from the Google Glass project. Analyze how Brin and the Google team navigated the technological, ethical, and social complexities of introducing a revolutionary device. Discuss the impact of Glass on the development of augmented reality technology and its influence on future Google endeavors.

Section 3: Life Sciences and Healthcare

Verily Life Sciences: A Technological Prescription

Shift the focus to Verily Life Sciences, a subsidiary of Alphabet Inc., dedicated to healthcare and life sciences. Explore Brin's interest in leveraging technology to transform healthcare, detailing initiatives such as the Baseline Study and the development of smart contact lenses for diabetes monitoring. Examine the intersection of technology and healthcare innovation.

Ethical Considerations in Health Tech

Address the ethical considerations surrounding Verily's healthcare initiatives. Discuss issues related to data privacy, the responsible use of technology in healthcare, and the challenges of navigating a landscape where innovation meets sensitive personal information. Illustrate how Brin's commitment to ethical innovation shapes Verily's approach.

Section 4: Beyond Alphabet: Other Ventures and Philanthropy

Sidewalk Labs and Urban Innovation

Explore Brin's involvement in Sidewalk Labs, an Alphabet subsidiary focused on urban innovation. Detail initiatives aimed at creating smart cities and leveraging technology to address urban challenges. Discuss the impact of these ventures on the urban landscape and the evolving role of technology in city planning.

Philanthropy: The Brin Wojcicki Foundation

Conclude the chapter by examining Sergey Brin's philanthropic endeavors through the Brin Wojcicki Foundation. Explore the causes and initiatives supported by the foundation, emphasizing Brin's commitment to using his wealth and influence for positive social impact. Illustrate how the foundation reflects Brin's broader vision for a better future.

Chapter 3 unravels Sergey Brin's visionary pursuits beyond Google, from moonshot projects to transformative ventures in healthcare, urban innovation, and philanthropy. It explores the intersection of technology and social impact, revealing Brin's commitment to pushing the boundaries of innovation for the betterment of society.

5

The Philosopher Coder: Sergey Brin's Ethical Stance in the Digital Age

Section 1: The Ethical Imperative

Beyond the Binary: Brin's Ethical Framework
Open the chapter by exploring Sergey Brin's philosophical foundations and the ethical framework that guides his approach to technology. Delve into Brin's early experiences, cultural influences, and the ethical considerations that shaped his perspective on the responsibilities of tech innovators.

The Power and Responsibility of Code
Examine Brin's belief in the power of code as a force for both progress and potential harm. Discuss his views on the ethical responsibilities that come with writing algorithms and creating technologies that shape the digital landscape. Illustrate how Brin's ethical stance has influenced Google's approach to product development and societal impact.

Section 2: The Open Web and Information Accessibility

The Democratization of Information

Explore Brin's commitment to an open and accessible web. Discuss Google's role in democratizing information and breaking down barriers to knowledge. Highlight initiatives such as Google Scholar and Google Books, showcasing how Brin's vision aligns with the ideal of a globally accessible repository of information.

Censorship and the Great Firewall

Address the ethical challenges Google faced in navigating issues of censorship, particularly in the context of its operations in countries with restrictive information policies. Examine the tensions between Google's mission to organize the world's information and the ethical complexities of complying with local laws that restrict access to certain content.

Section 3: Data Privacy and Security

The Balancing Act

Delve into Brin's perspective on the delicate balance between data-driven innovation and individual privacy. Explore Google's evolving approach to data privacy, from the early days to contemporary challenges. Discuss Brin's role in shaping policies that prioritize user privacy while still harnessing the power of data for innovation.

The Snowden Revelations

Examine the impact of Edward Snowden's revelations about government surveillance programs on Google and other tech companies. Discuss how Brin and Google responded to concerns about user privacy and government access to data. Illustrate the ethical dilemmas faced by tech companies in the era of mass surveillance.

Section 4: Artificial Intelligence and Ethical AI

The Rise of AI

Transition to the ethical considerations surrounding artificial intelligence (AI). Explore Brin's views on the responsible development and deployment of AI technologies. Discuss Google's AI principles, emphasizing transparency, fairness, and accountability in the design and use of AI systems.

Ethical Challenges in AI
Examine specific ethical challenges posed by the use of AI, such as bias in algorithms, the potential for job displacement, and the ethical implications of autonomous systems. Illustrate how Brin, Google, and the tech industry at large are addressing these challenges and striving to ensure that AI technologies benefit humanity.

Section 5: Legacy and Future Challenges

Defining a Legacy
Conclude the chapter by reflecting on Sergey Brin's evolving legacy in the technology industry. Discuss the lasting impact of his ethical principles on Google and the broader tech landscape. Explore the challenges that lie ahead in an era where technology's influence on society continues to grow and the responsibilities of tech leaders become increasingly complex.

Chapter 4 unravels the ethical considerations that have shaped Sergey Brin's journey as a tech visionary. From information accessibility to data privacy, and the ethical challenges of AI, this chapter explores the intricate balance Brin seeks to strike between technological innovation and societal responsibility in the digital age.

6

Sergey Brin: A Personal Odyssey Beyond Technology

Section 1: The Personal Side of Sergey Brin

Family and Relationships

Open the chapter with a glimpse into Sergey Brin's personal life. Explore his relationships with family and friends, shedding light on the human side of the tech mogul. Delve into how personal experiences, values, and relationships have influenced Brin's approach to life, business, and innovation.

A Life Unplugged

Explore Brin's lifestyle choices, including his interest in outdoor activities, adventure sports, and travel. Discuss how these pursuits provide a counterbalance to the demands of the tech industry and contribute to Brin's overall well-being. Illustrate how Brin's personal interests and passions shape his worldview beyond the confines of Silicon Valley.

Section 2: Challenges and Triumphs

Health Challenges

Address the public revelation of Sergey Brin's genetic predisposition to Parkinson's disease. Explore how Brin's commitment to personal health and wellness intersect with his philanthropic endeavors, particularly in the field of life sciences and healthcare. Discuss the challenges and triumphs associated with managing a high-profile career while facing health concerns.

Triumphs in the Skies

Shift the focus to Brin's fascination with aviation and his involvement in cutting-edge aviation projects. Explore his interest in space exploration, including investments in private space companies. Discuss how Brin's passion for aerospace ties into his broader vision for the future of technology and human exploration.

Section 3: Entrepreneurial Ventures

Beyond Google: Other Ventures

Explore Sergey Brin's involvement in various entrepreneurial ventures beyond Google. Highlight investments, start-ups, and projects that showcase Brin's diverse interests, from clean energy initiatives to biotechnology. Discuss how these ventures reflect Brin's entrepreneurial spirit and his commitment to addressing global challenges.

The Playground of Ideas: Area 120

Examine Brin's support for innovation within Google through initiatives like Area 120. Discuss how this internal incubator allows Google employees to explore and develop their entrepreneurial ideas. Illustrate how Brin fosters a culture of creativity and experimentation within the company.

Section 4: Reflections on Success and Impact

The Billionaire's Dilemma

Explore Brin's reflections on wealth, success, and the responsibilities that come with it. Discuss his views on philanthropy, wealth distribution, and the role of billionaires in addressing societal challenges. Illustrate how Brin's personal beliefs influence his approach to wealth and its impact on the world.

The Impact on Society

Conclude the chapter by reflecting on Sergey Brin's impact on society beyond technology. Discuss how his personal choices, values, and endeavors contribute to a broader conversation about the role of tech leaders in shaping the world. Explore the intersection of personal values, societal impact, and the legacy Brin envisions for himself and his contributions.

Chapter 5 delves into the personal dimensions of Sergey Brin's life, exploring his relationships, triumphs, challenges, and entrepreneurial ventures. It provides a holistic view of Brin as an individual, beyond his role as a tech innovator, offering insights into the factors that shape his worldview and his contributions beyond the digital realm.

7

Sergey Brin's Vision for Tomorrow: Navigating the Future Landscape

S ection 1: The Evolving Digital Landscape

Technology in Flux

Open the chapter with an overview of the rapidly evolving digital landscape. Discuss emerging technologies, trends, and shifts in user behavior that are reshaping the way people interact with technology. Set the stage for Sergey Brin's forward-looking vision in navigating this dynamic environment.

The Fourth Industrial Revolution

Explore Brin's perspective on the Fourth Industrial Revolution, emphasizing the convergence of digital, physical, and biological technologies. Discuss how Brin envisions the transformative impact of this revolution on industries, societies, and individuals, and his role in shaping this future.

Section 2: Artificial Intelligence and Machine Learning

AI's Transformative Potential

Delve into Brin's views on the future of artificial intelligence (AI) and machine learning. Explore how these technologies are poised to revolutionize industries, from healthcare to finance. Discuss the ethical considerations and societal implications of an AI-driven future, as well as Brin's role in steering these technologies responsibly.

Human-AI Collaboration

Illustrate Brin's vision for a harmonious collaboration between humans and AI. Explore initiatives and projects that aim to augment human capabilities, improve decision-making, and enhance overall well-being. Discuss how Brin envisions a future where AI becomes a powerful tool for positive societal impact.

Section 3: The Next Frontier: Space Exploration

Beyond Earth: The New Space Age

Shift the focus to Brin's interest in space exploration and the new frontiers of the cosmos. Explore the role of private space companies, including those supported by Brin, in advancing space exploration. Discuss the potential for commercial space travel, colonization of other planets, and the broader implications of humanity's expansion into space.

Earth and Beyond: A Dual Commitment

Highlight Brin's dual commitment to addressing challenges on Earth while exploring opportunities beyond. Discuss the integration of environmental sustainability, clean energy, and technological innovation in Brin's vision for a future where humanity balances progress with responsible stewardship of the planet.

Section 4: Challenges and Opportunities

Global Challenges and Tech Solutions

Examine how Brin envisions technology addressing global challenges, from climate change to healthcare disparities. Discuss the role of innovation, collaboration, and international cooperation in developing tech-driven solutions to some of the world's most pressing issues.

The Intersection of Ethics and Innovation

Explore Brin's continued commitment to ethical considerations in the development and deployment of new technologies. Discuss how he navigates the ethical challenges posed by emerging technologies and the importance of incorporating ethical principles into the fabric of innovation.

Section 5: Legacy and Continuity

Nurturing Future Innovators

Explore Brin's efforts to inspire and nurture the next generation of innovators. Discuss educational initiatives, mentorship programs, and investments in fostering a culture of curiosity, creativity, and ethical responsibility among aspiring technologists.

A Lasting Legacy

Conclude the chapter by reflecting on the legacy Sergey Brin envisions for himself and the impact he hopes to leave on the world. Discuss how his forward-looking vision aligns with a commitment to creating a future where technology serves humanity, fosters progress, and addresses the challenges of tomorrow.

Chapter 6 dives into Sergey Brin's vision for the future, exploring his insights on emerging technologies, space exploration, global challenges, and the ethical considerations that will shape the digital landscape. It offers a glimpse into the mind of a forward-thinking innovator, navigating the complexities of tomorrow's world.

8

Sergey Brin's Cultural Impact: Redefining Innovation and Leadership

Section 1: The Google Legacy

Google's Enduring Influence

Open the chapter by examining the lasting impact of Google on the tech industry, business, and society. Discuss how Google, co-founded by Sergey Brin, has become synonymous with innovation, information access, and user-centric design. Explore the ways in which Google has shaped the digital landscape and set new standards for tech companies.

The Google Culture

Delve into the unique culture fostered at Google under Brin's leadership. Discuss the emphasis on creativity, collaboration, and a supportive work environment. Explore how Google's culture of "moonshot thinking" and continuous innovation has become a model for other companies in Silicon Valley and beyond.

Section 2: Leadership Philosophy

Leadership by Example

Examine Sergey Brin's leadership style and philosophy. Discuss how his hands-on approach, intellectual curiosity, and commitment to a positive work culture have influenced Google's trajectory. Explore anecdotes and examples that illustrate Brin's leadership principles and their impact on the company's success.

Empowering Innovation

Highlight Brin's efforts to empower and inspire innovation within Google. Discuss initiatives, such as "20% time" and internal projects like Area 120, that encourage employees to pursue their passion projects. Explore how Brin's leadership fosters a sense of ownership and creativity among Google's diverse workforce.

Section 3: Diversity and Inclusion

Nurturing Diversity

Explore Brin's views on diversity and inclusion within the tech industry. Discuss the initiatives implemented at Google to promote diversity, including hiring practices, mentorship programs, and support for underrepresented groups. Illustrate how Brin's commitment to diversity aligns with his broader vision for a more inclusive and equitable future.

The Challenges of Inclusion

Examine the challenges and controversies Google has faced related to diversity and inclusion. Discuss how Brin and the company navigate these issues, learning from setbacks and continually striving to create an environment that reflects a diverse array of perspectives and talents.

Section 4: The Tech Philanthropist

Philanthropy and Social Impact

Shift the focus to Brin's philanthropic efforts and their impact on society.

Explore the initiatives supported by the Brin Wojcicki Foundation, emphasizing education, healthcare, and other areas of social impact. Discuss how Brin's philanthropy aligns with his values and contributes to a broader vision of positive change.

The Giving Pledge

Discuss Brin's involvement in the Giving Pledge, a commitment by some of the world's wealthiest individuals to donate a significant portion of their wealth to address societal challenges. Explore the motivations behind Brin's participation and the potential impact of such philanthropic endeavors on global issues.

Section 5: Reflections on Innovation

Lessons from the Journey

Conclude the chapter with reflections on the lessons learned from Sergey Brin's journey. Discuss how his approach to innovation, leadership, and philanthropy offers insights for aspiring entrepreneurs, tech leaders, and anyone seeking to make a positive impact on the world. Illustrate how Brin's legacy extends beyond technology into the realms of culture, leadership, and societal responsibility.

Chapter 7 explores Sergey Brin's cultural impact, examining how his leadership at Google, commitment to diversity and inclusion, and philanthropic endeavors have left an indelible mark on the tech industry and beyond. It reflects on the lessons learned from Brin's journey and his contributions to shaping a culture of innovation and positive change.

9

Sergey Brin: A Continuum of Curiosity and Impact

Section 1: The Ever-Curious Mind

Curiosity Unleashed

Open the chapter by delving into Sergey Brin's insatiable curiosity. Explore how his relentless pursuit of knowledge, exploration, and innovation has been a driving force throughout his career. Discuss anecdotes and pivotal moments that showcase Brin's curiosity as a guiding principle in his personal and professional life.

Lifelong Learning

Examine Brin's commitment to lifelong learning and intellectual growth. Discuss how he stays informed about diverse subjects, engages with new ideas, and encourages a culture of continuous learning within the organizations he influences. Illustrate the impact of intellectual curiosity on Brin's decision-making and problem-solving processes.

Section 2: The Tech Visionary's Evolution

Adapting to Change

Explore how Sergey Brin has adapted to the rapidly changing tech landscape. Discuss his ability to anticipate trends, pivot strategies, and embrace new technologies. Illustrate how Brin's foresight and adaptability have played a crucial role in sustaining his influence and impact over time.

Lessons from Setbacks

Examine instances where Brin faced challenges or setbacks in his career. Discuss how he navigated these moments, the lessons learned, and the resilience that propelled him forward. Illustrate the importance of overcoming obstacles in the pursuit of long-term goals.

Section 3: The Global Citizen

Beyond Borders

Explore Brin's identity as a global citizen and the impact of his international background on his worldview. Discuss his involvement in global initiatives, collaborations, and the ways in which he leverages technology to address challenges on a global scale. Illustrate how Brin's global perspective informs his vision for the future.

Bridging Cultures

Highlight Brin's efforts to bridge cultural gaps and foster collaboration across diverse communities. Discuss initiatives, partnerships, and projects that reflect Brin's commitment to creating a more interconnected and inclusive world. Illustrate how technology can serve as a tool for cultural understanding and collaboration.

Section 4: The Tech Mentor

Nurturing Talent

Explore Brin's role as a mentor and influencer in the tech industry. Discuss his interactions with emerging entrepreneurs, startup founders, and the next generation of tech leaders. Illustrate how Brin's guidance and mentorship contribute to the development of innovative ideas and sustainable businesses.

Fostering Innovation Ecosystems

Discuss Brin's efforts to support innovation ecosystems beyond his direct involvement in companies. Explore initiatives, investments, and collaborations aimed at fostering environments where creativity and entrepreneurship can flourish. Illustrate how Brin envisions a broader ecosystem of innovation that extends beyond individual companies.

Section 5: The Future Unveiled

Continuing the Journey

Conclude the chapter by exploring the future trajectory of Sergey Brin's journey. Discuss potential areas of focus, new ventures, and evolving interests. Illustrate how Brin's legacy is a continuum of exploration, impact, and an unwavering commitment to shaping a future where technology and humanity coalesce.

Chapter 8 encapsulates the ongoing narrative of Sergey Brin's journey, exploring his enduring curiosity, evolution as a tech visionary, global influence, mentorship role, and the unfolding chapters of his future endeavors. It paints a portrait of a leader whose impact transcends boundaries and continues to shape the landscape of technology and innovation.

10

Sergey Brin's Visionary Tapestry: Weaving Innovation into the Fabric of Tomorrow

Section 1: The Intersection of Technology and Humanity

Human-Centric Innovation

Open the chapter by exploring Sergey Brin's commitment to human-centric innovation. Discuss how he envisions technology as a tool to enhance the human experience, address societal challenges, and foster positive change. Illustrate instances where Brin's vision converges with the broader goals of creating technology that serves humanity.

The Ethical Imperative

Revisit the ethical considerations that have been a recurring theme in Brin's journey. Discuss how he continues to prioritize ethical principles in the development and deployment of technology. Illustrate initiatives and projects that reflect a commitment to responsible innovation, transparency, and the ethical use of data.

Section 2: Beyond Google: A Multifaceted Impact

The Legacy of Google

Reflect on Google's enduring legacy and its ongoing impact on the digital landscape. Discuss how the principles and culture established by Brin and Larry Page continue to shape the company's trajectory. Explore Google's influence on search, online platforms, and its contributions to the evolution of the internet.

Alphabet Inc.: A Diversified Vision

Examine the evolution of Alphabet Inc. and its diversified portfolio of ventures. Discuss how the restructuring has allowed Brin to pursue a wide range of interests, from moonshot projects to healthcare and beyond. Illustrate how Alphabet reflects Brin's vision for a company that embraces diverse innovations.

Section 3: Moonshots Revisited

The Legacy of Google X

Explore the lasting impact of Google X and its moonshot projects. Discuss the projects that have succeeded, the lessons learned from those that haven't, and how Google X continues to push the boundaries of what is possible. Illustrate how the spirit of moonshot thinking persists as a driving force within Alphabet.

The Unpredictable Future

Discuss Brin's views on the unpredictable nature of technological advancement. Explore his thoughts on anticipating the future, managing risks, and embracing uncertainty in the pursuit of groundbreaking ideas. Illustrate how Brin's approach to the unknown shapes his vision for the future.

Section 4: Bridging Innovation and Philanthropy

Tech for Good

Examine how Sergey Brin envisions technology as a force for good in philanthropy. Discuss projects and initiatives that leverage technology to address social issues, improve healthcare, and contribute to global well-being. Illustrate the interconnected nature of Brin's technological and philanthropic pursuits.

The Brin Wojcicki Foundation: A Catalyst for Change

Explore the ongoing impact of the Brin Wojcicki Foundation. Discuss the foundation's initiatives, partnerships, and contributions to education, healthcare, and other areas of societal impact. Illustrate how Brin's philanthropy complements his vision for positive change.

Section 5: Future Horizons

Uncharted Frontiers

Conclude the chapter by exploring the uncharted frontiers of Sergey Brin's vision. Discuss emerging technologies, potential areas of interest, and the evolving challenges and opportunities on the horizon. Illustrate how Brin's trajectory continues to be a tapestry of exploration, innovation, and a commitment to shaping a better future.

Chapter 9 serves as a culmination of Sergey Brin's visionary journey, weaving together themes of technology, ethics, innovation, and philanthropy. It explores the multifaceted impact of Brin's endeavors, reflecting on the legacy of Google, the ongoing influence of moonshot projects, and the evolving horizons of a tech pioneer shaping the fabric of tomorrow.

11

Sergey Brin: A Reflection on Innovation, Impact, and the Future

Section 1: Reflecting on the Journey

The Evolution of a Visionary

Open the chapter by reflecting on the transformative journey of Sergey Brin. Discuss key milestones, challenges, and defining moments that have shaped his trajectory. Illustrate how Brin's evolution as a visionary leader mirrors the rapid changes and advancements in the tech industry.

Lessons Learned

Explore the lessons learned from Brin's experiences and endeavors. Discuss the insights gained from successes, setbacks, and the continuous process of innovation. Illustrate how these lessons contribute to Brin's ongoing approach to leadership, technology, and the intersection of innovation and ethics.

Section 2: Impact on the Tech Landscape

Shaping the Digital Era

Examine the profound impact Sergey Brin has had on the tech landscape. Discuss how Google, Alphabet, and Brin's visionary contributions have reshaped how people access information, interact with technology, and envision the future of innovation. Illustrate the enduring legacy of his influence.

The Ripple Effect

Explore the ripple effect of Brin's innovations on the broader tech ecosystem. Discuss how Google's success and the principles championed by Brin have influenced other companies, startups, and entrepreneurs. Illustrate how the culture of innovation he cultivated continues to inspire the next generation of tech leaders.

Section 3: The Societal Impact

Technology and Society

Reflect on the societal impact of Brin's technological contributions. Discuss how Google's products and services have become integral parts of daily life for billions of people worldwide. Illustrate how these technological advancements have influenced communication, information access, and societal norms.

Navigating Ethical Challenges

Revisit the ethical challenges Brin has faced and how he navigated them. Discuss the evolving landscape of ethical considerations in the tech industry and how Brin's commitment to responsible innovation has influenced the broader conversation around technology and ethics.

Section 4: The Future Unfolding

Continuing the Journey

Explore how Sergey Brin envisions the future of technology, innovation, and his own journey. Discuss his thoughts on the evolving role of AI, space exploration, and other emerging technologies. Illustrate the ongoing commitment to pushing the boundaries of what is possible in the pursuit of a better future.

The Tech Legacy

Reflect on the legacy Sergey Brin is shaping within the tech industry. Discuss how his impact extends beyond individual companies, influencing the broader landscape of technology and innovation. Illustrate how his legacy reflects a commitment to ethical leadership, continuous learning, and a dedication to positive societal impact.

Section 5: A Call to Action

Inspiring Future Innovators

Conclude the chapter with a call to action. Discuss how Brin's journey can inspire future innovators, entrepreneurs, and leaders to approach challenges with curiosity, resilience, and an ethical mindset. Illustrate the potential for positive change when technology is harnessed responsibly for the betterment of humanity.

Chapter 10 serves as a reflective conclusion to Sergey Brin's journey, exploring the impact he has had on the tech landscape, society, and the ethical considerations that accompany innovation. It looks toward the future, offering insights and inspiration for those who will shape the next chapters of the ever-evolving tech narrative.

12

Beyond the Horizon: The Ongoing Legacy of Sergey Brin

Section 1: A Continued Exploration

A New Chapter

Open the chapter by exploring the latest developments and endeavors in Sergey Brin's journey. Discuss any recent projects, initiatives, or shifts in focus that highlight the ongoing evolution of his vision. Illustrate how Brin continues to explore new frontiers in technology and innovation.

Collaborations and Partnerships

Examine Brin's collaborations and partnerships with other industry leaders, organizations, or research institutions. Discuss how these collaborations contribute to the exchange of ideas, the advancement of technology, and the potential for solving complex challenges on a global scale.

Section 2: Tech and Beyond

Emerging Technologies

Delve into Brin's perspective on emerging technologies. Discuss how he views advancements in fields such as artificial intelligence, biotechnology, or quantum computing. Illustrate how Brin's ongoing interest in cutting-edge technologies shapes his outlook on the future.

The Intersection of Tech and Humanity

Explore how Brin continues to navigate the delicate balance between technology and humanity. Discuss his thoughts on ensuring that technological progress aligns with ethical considerations, human values, and the betterment of society. Illustrate how he envisions the symbiotic relationship between technology and human flourishing.

Section 3: Philanthropy and Social Impact

Continued Philanthropic Endeavors

Examine the ongoing philanthropic initiatives supported by Sergey Brin. Discuss how his foundation, the Brin Wojcicki Foundation, continues to contribute to education, healthcare, and other areas of social impact. Illustrate the lasting impact of these initiatives on communities and individuals.

Addressing Global Challenges

Explore Brin's perspective on addressing global challenges through philanthropy and technology. Discuss his views on leveraging resources, technology, and collaborative efforts to tackle pressing issues such as climate change, healthcare disparities, or access to education on a global scale.

Section 4: Mentorship and Education

Nurturing Talent

Reflect on Brin's role as a mentor and contributor to the development of future innovators. Discuss mentorship programs, educational initiatives, or investments aimed at fostering a new generation of thinkers and leaders in technology and beyond.

Educational Initiatives

Explore Brin's involvement in educational initiatives, whether through partnerships with educational institutions, support for STEM programs, or other efforts to inspire and equip the next wave of learners and innovators.

Section 5: Reflections on a Lasting Legacy

The Evergreen Impact

Reflect on the evergreen impact of Sergey Brin's legacy. Discuss how his contributions have stood the test of time and continue to shape the tech industry, inspire innovation, and influence the ethical considerations surrounding technology.

Beyond Individuals: Shaping a Future Together

Conclude the chapter by reflecting on how Brin's legacy extends beyond an individual's impact. Discuss the collective responsibility of tech leaders, innovators, and society at large in shaping a future where technology is a force for positive change, guided by ethical principles.

Chapter 11 provides a contemporary view of Sergey Brin's ongoing legacy, exploring recent developments, collaborations, and the continued impact of his work in technology, philanthropy, and education. It highlights how Brin's journey remains dynamic and relevant in the ever-evolving landscape of innovation.

13

The Future Unveiled: Sergey Brin's Enduring Vision for Tomorrow

Section 1: Navigating Uncharted Territories

The Ever-Expanding Horizon

Open the chapter by exploring the uncharted territories that Sergey Brin continues to navigate. Discuss any recent ventures, projects, or futuristic endeavors that exemplify Brin's commitment to pushing the boundaries of innovation. Illustrate how his vision remains forward-looking and adaptive to the evolving technological landscape.

Technological Frontiers

Delve into Brin's perspectives on emerging technological frontiers. Discuss how he envisions the future of technology, including the potential impact of developments in fields such as artificial intelligence, biotechnology, quantum computing, or other cutting-edge areas. Illustrate Brin's role in shaping the trajectory of these advancements.

Section 2: Ethical Leadership in a Digital Age

A Legacy of Ethical Leadership

Reflect on how Sergey Brin's legacy as an ethical leader continues to evolve. Discuss recent instances where ethical considerations played a crucial role in decision-making, product development, or corporate policies within companies influenced by Brin. Illustrate how he addresses the ongoing challenges of navigating ethical dilemmas in a rapidly evolving digital age.

Ethical Tech Advocacy

Explore Brin's advocacy for ethical practices within the tech industry. Discuss his role in influencing broader conversations about responsible technology use, data privacy, and the societal impact of emerging technologies. Illustrate how Brin's ethical stance contributes to shaping industry standards and expectations.

Section 3: Shaping Societal Impact

Global Philanthropy in Action

Examine the current state of philanthropic initiatives supported by Sergey Brin. Discuss recent projects, partnerships, or innovations funded by the Brin Wojcicki Foundation and their impact on addressing societal challenges. Illustrate how Brin's philanthropic efforts extend beyond financial contributions to actively shaping solutions.

Social Innovation

Explore Brin's perspective on social innovation and its role in addressing pressing global issues. Discuss how he envisions the intersection of technology, innovation, and social impact as a catalyst for positive change. Illustrate recent examples of social innovation initiatives aligned with Brin's vision.

Section 4: Mentorship and Fostering Innovation

Cultivating Future Leaders

Reflect on Brin's continued involvement in mentorship and fostering innovation. Discuss recent initiatives or programs aimed at nurturing talent, inspiring creativity, and supporting the development of future leaders in technology and related fields.

Incubating Ideas

Explore how Brin continues to foster a culture of experimentation and idea incubation. Discuss recent projects within organizations influenced by Brin that showcase a commitment to cultivating a creative and innovative work environment.

Section 5: Legacy in Flux

Adapting to Change

Examine how Sergey Brin's legacy adapts to the evolving dynamics of the tech industry and society. Discuss his approach to change, resilience in the face of challenges, and the ongoing impact of his legacy on the organizations he has shaped.

Beyond Individual Legacies

Conclude the chapter by reflecting on the broader implications of individual legacies in the tech industry. Discuss how the collective impact of leaders like Sergey Brin contributes to shaping a collective technological future and the shared responsibility of the industry in navigating this future together.

Chapter 12 unveils the present and future aspects of Sergey Brin's enduring vision, exploring recent developments, his ethical leadership, philanthropic contributions, and ongoing efforts to shape innovation and mentorship. It reflects on the evolving legacy of a tech pioneer and the collective responsibility of the industry in shaping the technological landscape of tomorrow.

14

Summary

Throughout the chapters, the narrative follows Sergey Brin's extraordinary journey from a young coder with a passion for technology to a co-founder of Google and a visionary shaping the future of innovation. The chapters delve into key themes such as Brin's early influences, the founding and growth of Google, his ethical considerations in technology, personal pursuits, and his expansive vision for the future. The narrative highlights his impact on the tech industry, society, and his commitment to philanthropy, mentorship, and responsible innovation. As the story unfolds, it captures Brin's ongoing exploration of new frontiers, ethical leadership, societal impact, and the enduring legacy he is crafting in the ever-evolving landscape of technology.

www.ingramcontent.com/pod-product-compliance
Lightning Source LLC
LaVergne TN
LVHW020455080526
838202LV00057B/5975